Official Songs of the United States Armed Forces

5 Piano Solos and a Medley

Arranged by Mary K. Sallee

Every day, countless stories of heroism are told about the men and women who serve in the United States Armed Forces. Their contributions play a vital role in maintaining peace, safety, and freedom throughout the world. To honor these remarkable individuals, this collection gathers into one volume the official songs of the Armed Forces. To make them accessible to pianists at various levels, arrangements are available in three separate editions:

- early intermediate to intermediate
- intermediate to late intermediate
- early advanced

The United States Armed Forces consist of five branches: the (1) Army, (2) Marine Corps, (3) Navy, (4) Air Force, and (5) Coast Guard. Each branch has a unique history and official song. This collection contains early advanced solo piano arrangements of the five songs, as well as a special concert-worthy medley that combines them. The arrangements are written in singable keys and contain lyrics, which makes them perfect for sing-alongs. They can also be performed for school talent shows, community celebrations, homecomings, and pageants. When played officially, the songs are to be performed in the order they are presented in this book.

"The Caissons Go Rolling Along" (aka "The Army Goes Rolling Along") was originally written by field artillery First Lieutenant Edmund L. Gruber, while he was stationed in the Philippines in 1908. It was transformed into a march by John Philip Sousa in 1917, and in 1956 it was adopted as the official song of the Army.

The **"Marines' Hymn"** is the oldest official song in the United States military. The author of the lyrics is unknown, but the music is from a duet in the 1859 opera *Geneviève de Brabant* by Jacques Offenbach.

"Anchors Aweigh" was written by Lieutenant Charles A. Zimmermann, bandmaster of the Naval Academy Band, and Midshipman First Class Alfred Hart Miles in 1906. It was subsequently dedicated to the Naval Academy Class of 1907 and adopted as the official song of the U.S. Navy. The word *weigh* comes from the archaic word meaning to heave, hoist, or raise. *Aweigh* means that the action has been completed. The anchor is aweigh when it is pulled from the bottom.

"The U.S. Air Force" (originally titled "Army Air Corps") was written by Robert MacArthur Crawford in 1938. It was one of hundreds of submissions to a song competition created by the Air Corps and sponsored by *Liberty* magazine.

Captain Francis Saltus Van Boskerck wrote the words to **"Semper Paratus"** in the cabin of the cutter Yamacraw in Savannah, Georgia, in 1922. He wrote the music five years later on a "beat-up old piano" in Unalaska, Alaska. The phrase *Semper Paratus* dates back to ancient times and means *always ready* or *ever ready.*

CONTENTS

Branch	Song Title	Page
The Army	The Caissons Go Rolling Along (aka "The Army Goes Rolling Along")	2
The Marine Corps	The Marines' Hymn (aka "From the Halls of Montezuma")	7
The Navy	Anchors Aweigh	12
The Air Force	The U.S. Air Force (aka "The Wild Blue Yonder")	20
The Coast Guard	Semper Paratus (Always Ready)	26
	Songs of the Armed Forces (A Medley for Solo Piano)	31

Produced by
Alfred Music
P.O. Box 10003
Van Nuys, CA 91410-0003
alfred.com

Printed in USA.

ISBN-10: 1-4706-2608-X
ISBN-13: 978-1-4706-2608-2

The Caissons Go Rolling Along

(aka "The Army Goes Rolling Along")

Words and Music by Edmund L. Gruber
Arr. Mary K. Sallee

caissons go rolling along. *poco rit.* First to

a tempo fight for the right and to build the nation's might. And the

Army goes rolling along. Proud of

all we have done, fighting till the battle's won. And the

Army goes rolling along. For it's

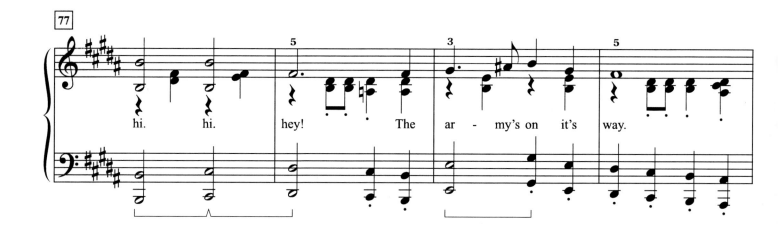

hi.   hi.   hey!   The ar - my's on   it's way.

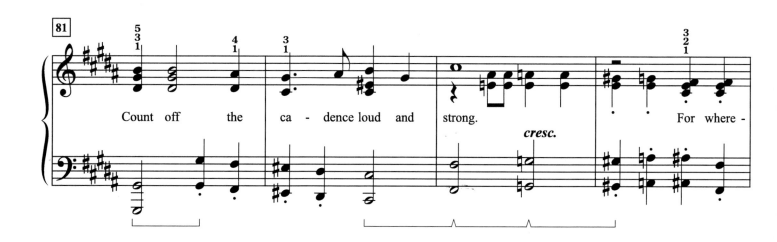

Count off   the   ca - dence loud and   strong.   *cresc.*   For where -

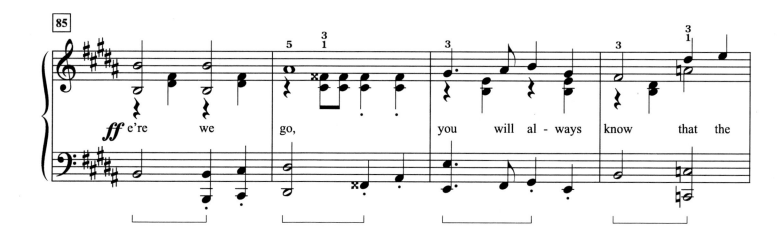

ff e're   we   go,   you   will al - ways know   that the

Ar - my   goes   roll - ing   a - long.   *sfz*

The Marines' Hymn
(aka "From the Halls of Montezuma")

Traditional
Arr. Mary K. Sallee

scenes._____ You will find us al - ways on the job, the U - nit - ed States Ma - rines.

cresc.

f

Here's____ health to you and to our Corps which____ we are proud to serve. In____

Anchors Aweigh

Music by Charles A. Zimmerman
Words by Alfred Hart Miles
Arr. Mary K. Sallee

sail   at   break   of   day,   day,   day,   day.
cresc.

ff Through   our   last   night   on   shore,

drink   to   the   foam.   Un -   til   we   meet   once   more: Here's

wish - ing   you   a   hap - py   voy - age   home.

The U.S. Air Force
(aka "The Wild Blue Yonder")

Words and Music by Robert Crawford
Arr. Mary K. Sallee

Fly - ing men,_____ guard-ing our na - tion's bor - ders,

f *cresc. poco a poco*

we'll be there,_____ ev - er on course!_____ In

ff

ech - e - lon,_____ we car - ry on, hey!

Noth-ing 'll stop the U. S. Air Force.

sfz

Semper Paratus
(Always Ready)

By Captain Francis Saltus Van Boskerck
Arr. Mary K. Sallee

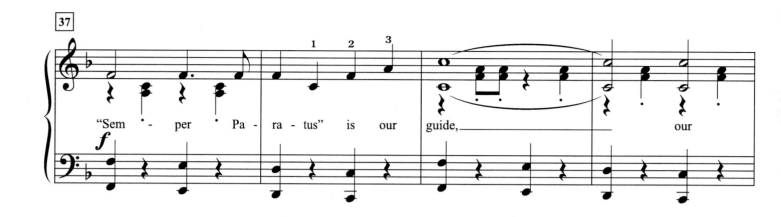

"Sem - per Pa - ra - tus" is our guide,_____ _____ our

fame, and glo - ry too._____ _____ To

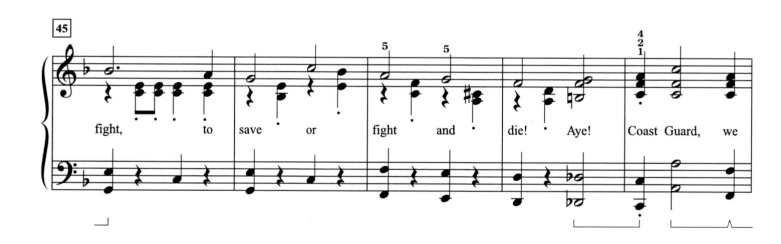

fight, to save or fight and die! Aye! Coast Guard, we

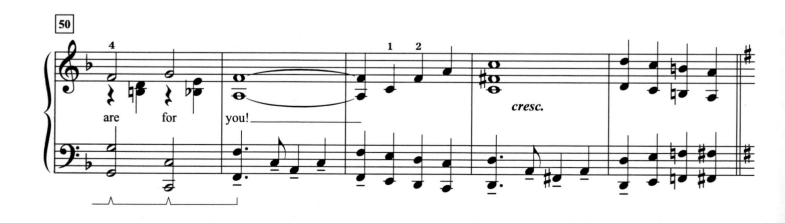

are for you!_____ _____ cresc.

We're al - ways read - y for the call, ___ we

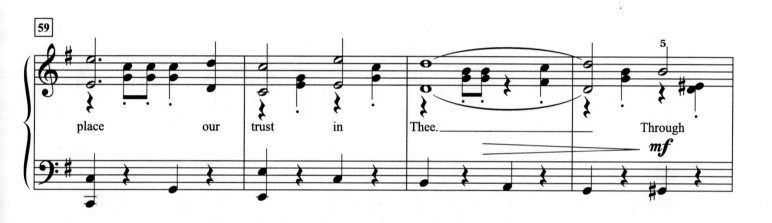

place our trust in Thee. ___ Through

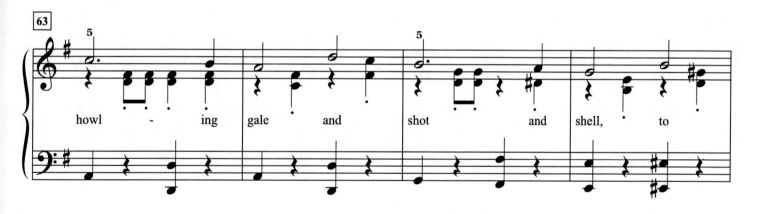

howl - ing gale and shot and shell, to

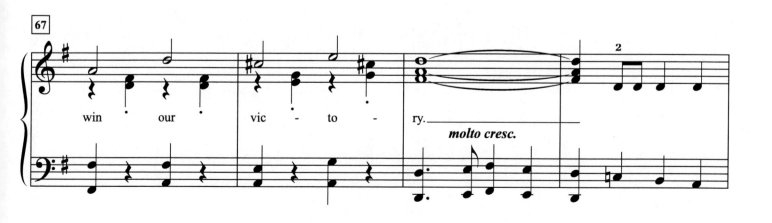

win our vic - to - ry. ___

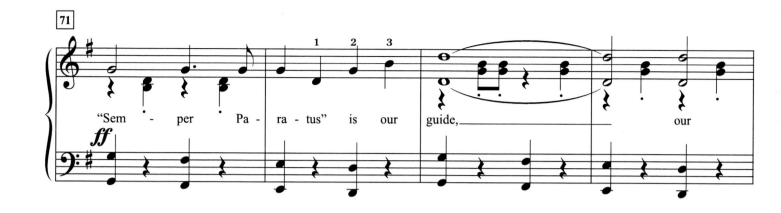

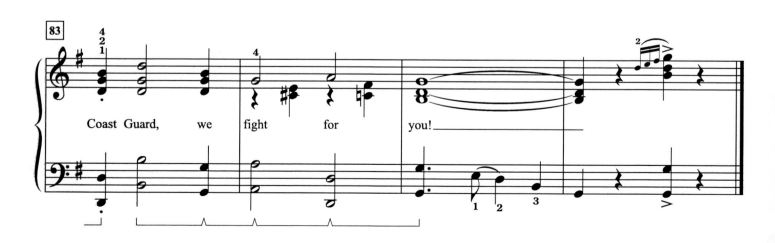

Songs of the Armed Forces
(A Medley for Solo Piano)

Arr. Mary K. Sallee

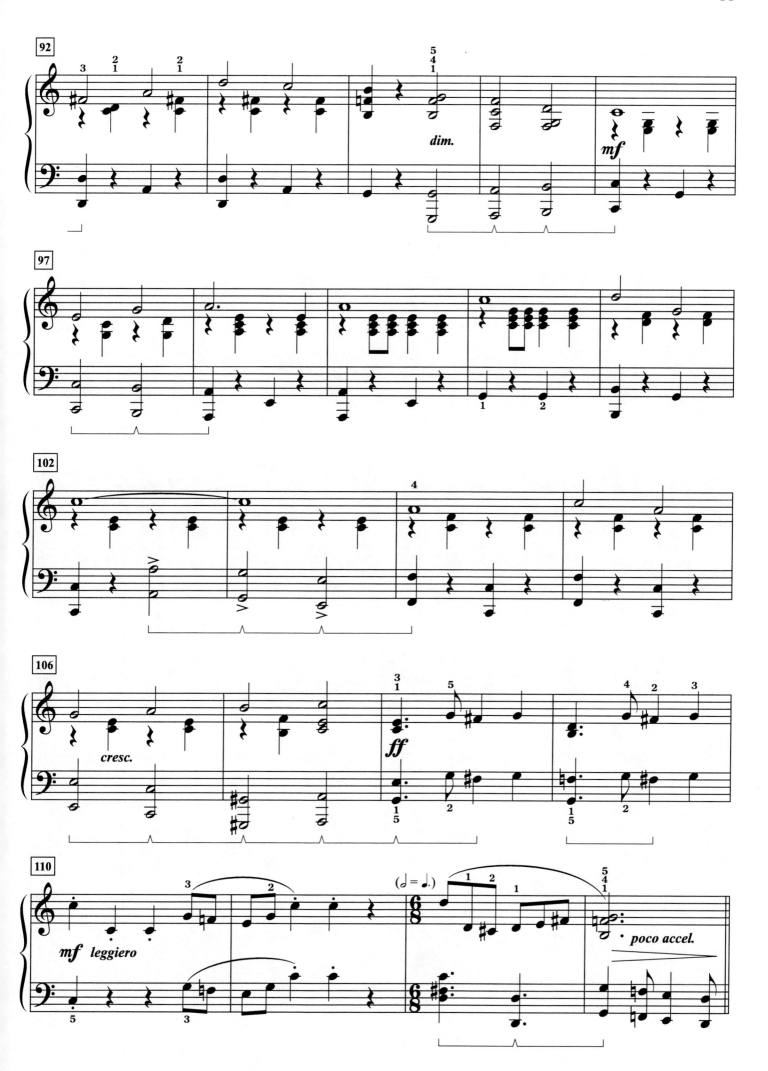

With gusto (♩. = 112)

114 *The U.S. Air Force (aka "The Wild Blue Yonder")*

"Semper Paratus"
By Captain Francis Saltus Van Boskerck
© 1938 (Renewed) WB MUSIC CORP.
All Rights Reserved